WHY SAM HOUSTON MATTERS TO TEXAS

By Lynn Peppas

Published in 2014 by The Rosen Publishing Group, Inc.
29 East 21st Street, New York, NY 10010

First Edition

Developed, written, and produced by Digital Discovery Publishing
Editors: Molly Aloian, Wendy Scavuzzo
Design & Production: Katherine Berti
Photo research: Crystal Sikkens
Proofreader: Sarah Cairns

Photo Credits: Everett Collection: 1
San Jacinto Museum of History: 7 (top)
Library of Congress: 9, 12, 15 (top), 19 (bottom); Copyright by J.D. Roberts: 9
Wikimedia Commons: Holley (Armstrong & Plaskitt): 10; cliff1066: 11 (bottom); Photograph by J. Williams: 13 (top); Texas State Library and Archives Commission: 16; Library of Congress collection: 24; The White House Historical Association: 24
Courtesy of the Star of the Republic Museum: 13 (bottom)
Shutterstock: 14
The Bridgeman Art Library : The Stapleton Collection : 15 (bottom); Dallas Historical Society, Texas, USA: 17
© North Wind / North Wind Picture Archives: 20 (top), 26
Smithsonian American Art Museum, Gift of Mrs. Joseph Harrison, Jr.: 20 (bottom), 21
Courtesy of Special Collections University of Houston Library, UH: 19 (top), 22
Illustration courtesy of harpersweekly.com: 27 (bottom)
Digital Discovery Publishing: 28 (bottom), 29
Katherine Berti: black and white image colorization, 5, 6, 12 (bottom), 23

All websites were live and accurate at the time of printing.

Library of Congress Cataloging-in-Publication Data

Peppas, Lynn.
Why Sam Houston matters to Texas / by Lynn Peppas.
p. cm. -- (Texas perspectives)
Includes index.
ISBN 978-1-4777-0912-2 (library binding)
ISBN 978-1-4777-0930-6 (pbk.)
ISBN 978-1-4777-0931-3 (6-pack)
1. Houston, Sam, -- 1793-1863 -- Juvenile literature. 2. Governors -- Texas -- Biography -- Juvenile literature. 3. Legislators -- United States -- Biography -- Juvenile literature. 4. Texas -- History -- To 1846 -- Juvenile literature. I. Peppas, Lynn. II. Title.
F390.H84 P47 2014
976.4--dc23

Manufactured in the United States of America

CPSIA Compliance Information: Batch W13PK: For Further Information contact Rosen Publishing, New York, New York at 1-800-237-9932

CONTENTS

1 WORDS OF WARNING

On a winter day in 1861, thousands of Texans gathered in Austin to hear Texas governor Sam Houston speak. Sam was well known in Texas. He was a military hero. He had been elected president of the Republic of Texas twice. Texans had, for many years, been happy to hear Sam's words. On this day, though, many Texans did not agree with what Sam had to say.

IMPERFECT UNION

At this time, many Americans were arguing over the issue of slavery. Northern states passed laws that banned slavery. Southern states, including Texas, did not want to ban slavery. Southern states began holding meetings, called **conventions**, to discuss **seceding**, or leaving, the **Union** with the United States. They wanted to form a new country, called the Confederate States of America, that allowed slavery. Sam warned of a bad outcome if Texas left the United States.

▼ *Sam was a leader in Texas for more than 25 years. He served as commander of the army, president of the Republic, senator, and governor.*

Sam spoke these words to the crowd gathered in Austin on February 23, 1861:

"Some of you laugh to scorn the idea of bloodshed as the result of secession. But let me tell you what is coming.... Your fathers and husbands, your sons and brothers, will be herded at the point of the bayonet...."

Sam was warning Texans that the southern states could never win a war against the Union, but the people would not listen. Sam had served Texans for many years. Now, though, the people he had fought and worked so hard for turned their backs on him.

Texas Perspective

Sam's motto was "Do right and risk consequences." He did what he felt was right, not what was popular.

SAM HOUSTON'S TEXAS

2 GROWING UP

Sam Houston was born on March 2, 1793, at Timber Ridge in Rockbridge County, Virginia. He was named after his father, Samuel. Sam's father was a major in the military. His mother, Elizabeth, ran the family farm with the help of African-American slaves. Sam had a large family. He had five brothers and three sisters.

TENNESSEE BOUND

By 1806, the Houston family had fallen on hard times. They sold their farm and most of their belongings. Sam's father died shortly before the sale. In 1807, Sam's mother packed up two wagons with the few possessions they had left and moved the family to a new farm on Baker Creek, in Tennessee.

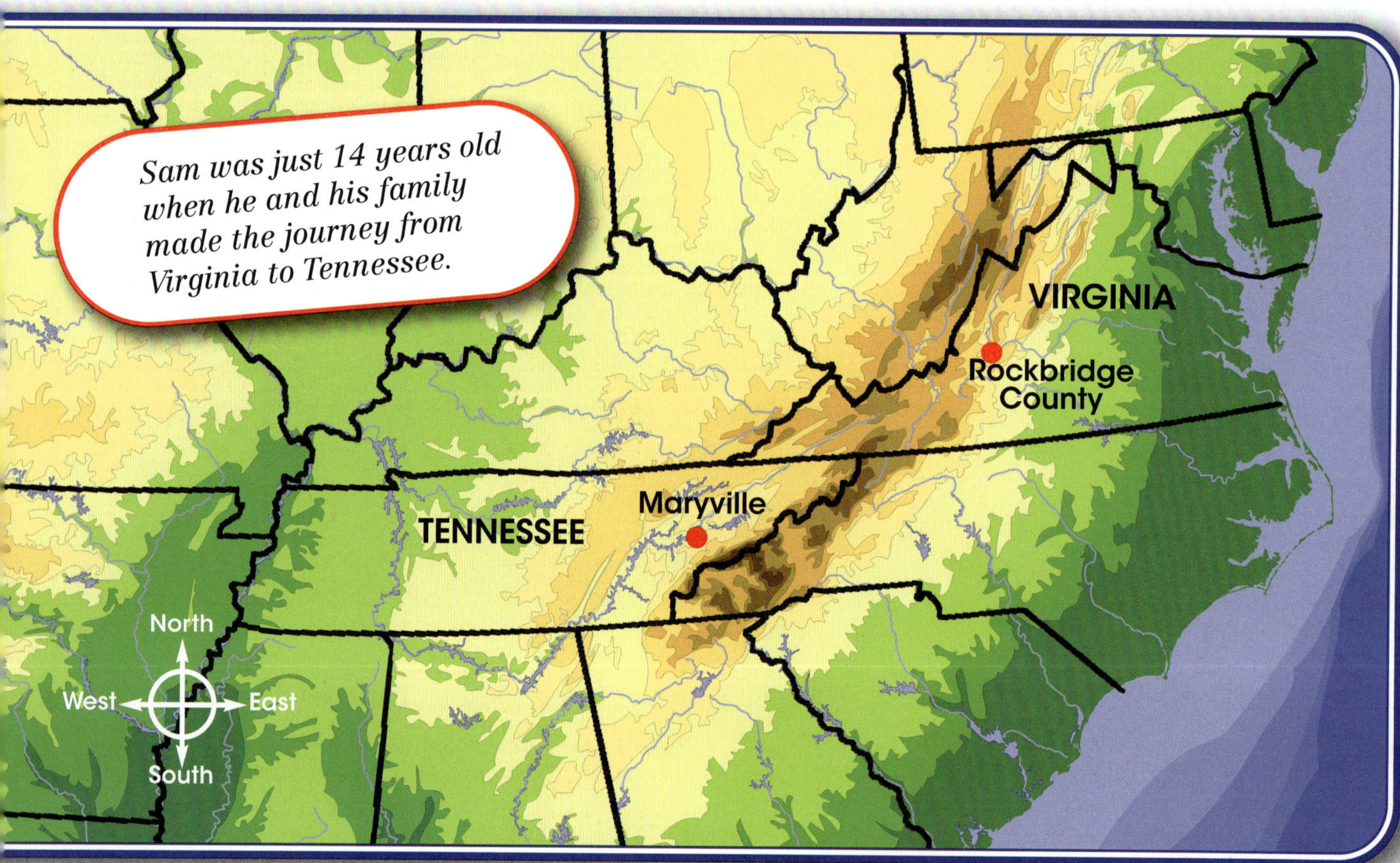

RUNAWAY

The Houston family worked on the farm in Tennessee and owned part of a general store in nearby Maryville. Sam did not like working on the farm or at the store. In 1809, at age 16, Sam ran away from home. His brothers went to look for him and found Sam living with a community of Cherokee Indians nearby. Sam told his brothers he liked living with the Cherokee and decided to stay.

▲ *As a youth Sam Houston enjoyed reading books on history and geography.*

ADOPTED

At a time when many people feared and disliked Native Americans, Sam made his home with them for almost three years. Sam learned about Cherokee traditions and **culture**, and was accepted into the community. They gave Sam the name Colonneh, which means "the raven" in English. The raven is an important part of Cherokee mythology.

▼ *A raven is a large black bird found throughout the United States.*

Sam is shown here with his adoptive father, Cherokee leader Chief Oolooteka. Chief Oolooteka was responsible for teaching Sam bravery and leadership skills that were useful later in his life.

BRAVERY IN WAR

In 1812, Sam returned to his family home from the Cherokee camp. That year, the Americans declared war against the British. Sam joined the US Army during the War of 1812.

Sam led an **infantry** unit under the command of General Andrew Jackson. General Jackson admired Sam's bravery and the two became friends. After the war, Sam asked for a job as an Indian agent. An Indian agent acted as a **go-between** for Indians and the US government. Jackson put in a good word for Sam and he got the job.

Sam was wounded several times during the war and nearly died. During the Battle of Horseshoe Bend, he ordered another soldier to pull an arrow from his leg.

General Andrew Jackson was a hero of the War of 1812. Jackson was also elected president of the United States in 1828.

A NEW CAREER

In the years that followed, Sam became a lawyer in Tennessee. His good friend Andrew Jackson also helped him begin a political career. In 1823, Sam was elected to Congress, and he was elected governor of Tennessee in 1827.

Sam's popularity in Tennessee was on the rise. He fell in love with a young woman named Eliza Allen, and they were married on January 22, 1829. The young couple had problems just a few months after their marriage and Eliza moved back to her parents' home. The breakup caused a scandal that ruined Sam's reputation. He quit his job as governor of Tennessee and went back to his Cherokee family.

▲ *As governor of Tennessee, Sam would sometimes dress in Cherokee clothing.*

AN IDEA

The Cherokee had been forced west from their homes in Tennessee. Chief Oolooteka and his tribe were living in what is now Arkansas, which shared part of its border with Texas. At that time, Texas was part of Mexico. While Sam was living with the Cherokee, an idea began to grow in his mind. He wanted Texas to become a state and join the United States.

Texas Perspective

Sam respected the rights of Indians and tried to maintain peaceful and fair dealings with them.

GONE TO TEXAS

In the 1820s, Texas was part of Mexico. At the time, **Anglo-American** settlers moved to Texas to receive land and start new lives. New settlers had to become citizens of Mexico and practice the **Roman Catholic** religion. By 1830, there were thousands of Anglo-American settlers living in Texas, along with their slaves. In 1830, the Mexican government made new laws to stop more Americans and their slaves from entering Texas. The Mexican government placed soldiers at military posts throughout Texas. The settlers were upset with the new laws so they organized meetings, called conventions, to complain.

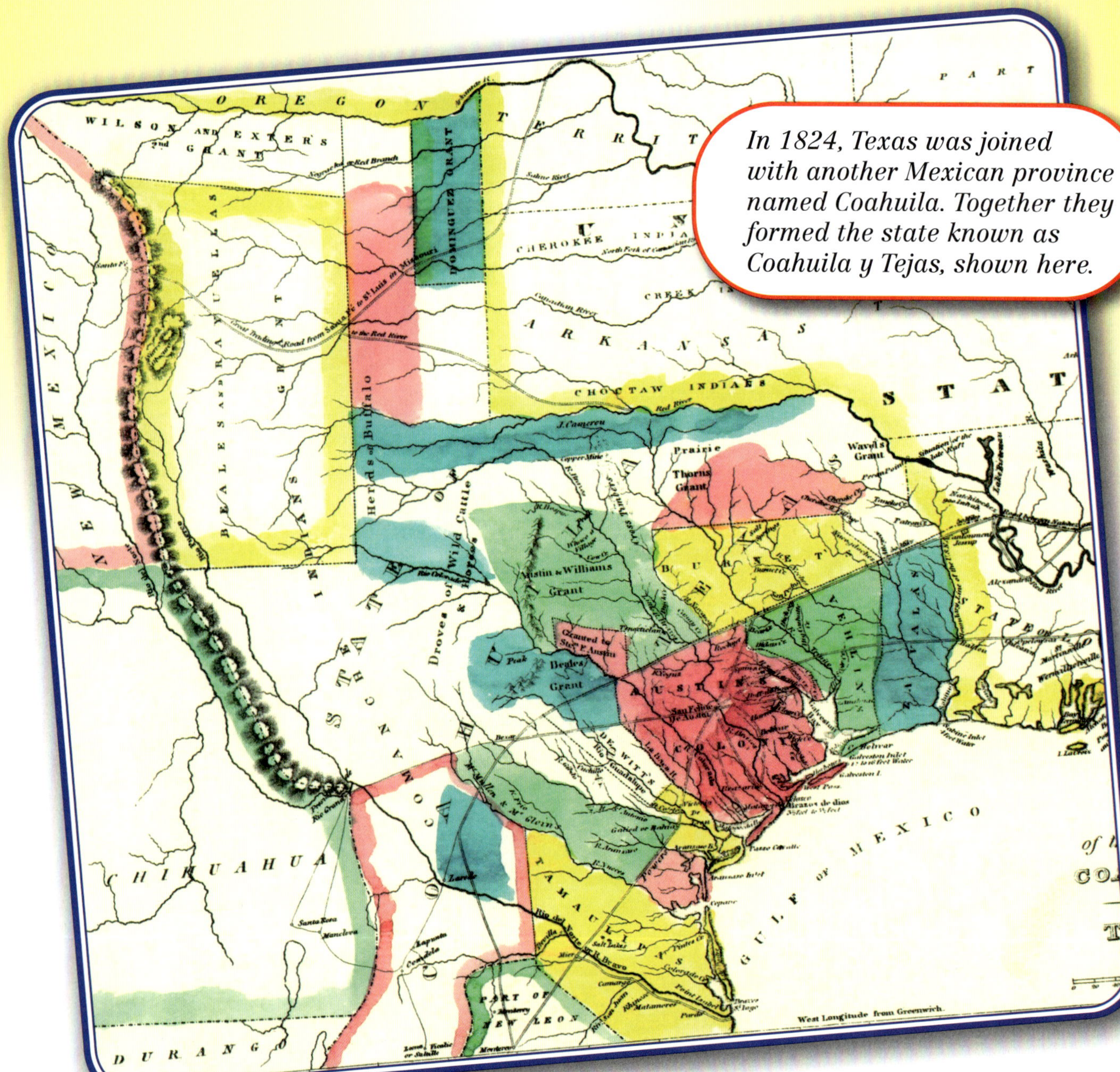

In 1824, Texas was joined with another Mexican province named Coahuila. Together they formed the state known as Coahuila y Tejas, shown here.

NEW CONSTITUTION

In December 1832, Sam Houston moved to Nacogdoches, Texas, and began to work as a lawyer. Anglo Americans living in Nacogdoches elected Sam as a **delegate** to the Convention of 1833. During the convention, delegates wrote a new state **constitution**. The constitution outlined Texans' desire for their own state government. They wanted to remain under the control of Mexico, but be separate from the Mexican state of Coahuila.

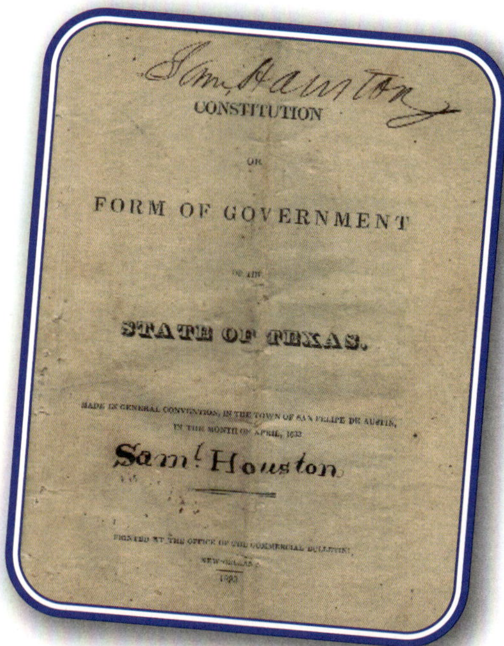
Sam Houston

CONSTITUTION

OR

FORM OF GOVERNMENT

OF THE

STATE OF TEXAS.

MADE IN GENERAL CONVENTION, IN THE TOWN OF SAN FELIPE DE AUSTIN, IN THE MONTH OF APRIL, 1833

Saml Houston

▲ *Much of the constitution of 1833 is believed to be in Sam Houston's own handwriting.*

MEXICO SAYS NO

Stephen F. Austin, who was president of the convention, delivered the new constitution to government officials in Mexico City in July 1833. The Mexican government did not agree with the Texans' demands and put Austin in prison. He was treated harshly, but was never charged or given a trial. Mexican president Antonio López de Santa Anna finally released him after almost one year. When he returned to Texas in September 1835, Austin told the settlers, "War is our only **recourse**." Austin did not want Texas to go to war with Mexico. However he felt war was the only way Texas would become independent.

Stephen F. Austin was responsible for bringing the first Anglo-American settlers to Texas in 1821.

3 REVOLUTION!

In 1835, Mexican president Antonio López de Santa Anna sent the army to Texas to oversee and control the people. Some Texans joined the Peace Party because they did not want war. Others joined the War Party because they wanted to fight for Texas independence. Sam Houston knew that a war with Mexico was coming.

BATTLE OF GONZALES

While Sam Houston and other leaders were deciding what to do about Mexico, Mexican troops marched to Gonzales, Texas. They planned to take back a cannon that Mexico had given the Texans to defend themselves against Indian attacks. A small fight, called the Battle of Gonzales, took place on October 2, 1835, between the Mexican army and the Texas soldiers commanded by Stephen Austin. The Mexican army was outnumbered and retreated. It was the first battle between Texas and Mexico in the Texas Revolution.

Mexican president Antonio López de Santa Anna often went into battle with his troops.

◀Texans in Gonzales raised a flag to anger the Mexican troops. The flag featured a painted image of a cannon, a lone star, and the words "Come and take it."

INDEPENDENCE!

On March 2, 1836, Sam served as a delegate at another convention. During the convention, Sam was appointed major general of the Texas army. The Texas Declaration of Independence was created during this convention, too. The Declaration accused the Mexican government of not protecting the lives, freedoms, and property of its citizens living in Texas. As a result, Texas declared its independence from Mexico and became a republic. A republic is a country that is usually run by a president or elected ruler.

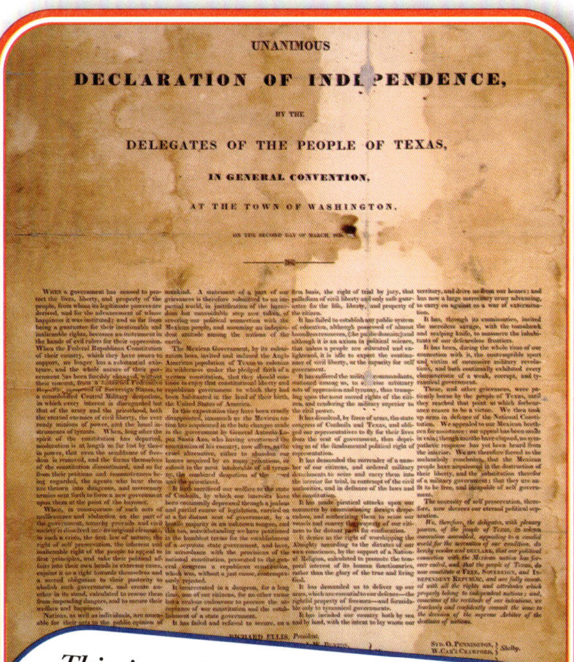
UNANIMOUS

DECLARATION OF INDEPENDENCE,

BY THE

DELEGATES OF THE PEOPLE OF TEXAS,

IN GENERAL CONVENTION,

AT THE TOWN OF WASHINGTON.

This is a photo of the Texas Declaration of Independence. It was adopted on March 2, which was also Sam Houston's birthday.

In this painting, the 54 delegates at the convention listen as the Texas Declaration of Independence is read.

THE ALAMO

After Texas declared independence in the spring of 1836, Antonio López de Santa Anna and the Mexican army marched toward San Antonio. Sam Houston feared Mexican forces would attack the Mission San Antonio de Valero, more commonly known as the Alamo. Sam knew the Alamo was not properly protected. In a letter to his troops, he ordered them to abandon the Alamo. Sam's orders were ignored.

From the book *The Life of Sam Houston*, published in 1855:

> ***Houston...had given orders to the commanding officer to abandon and blow up the Alamo; but his orders had been disobeyed by the officer, and treated with contempt by the General Council, who had ordered the commander to defend the place to the last, promising to reinforce him.***

Santa Anna and his army reached San Antonio on February 23, 1836. On March 6, Santa Anna attacked the Alamo with about 1,800 soldiers. After 90 minutes of fierce fighting, only seven Texans were still alive. They were executed by Santa Anna's men shortly after. Texas lost about 189 men that day. Mexico's losses were far greater, with about 600 soldiers wounded or killed in the battle.

The Alamo was important because it was located on a main road into the heart of Texas.

The Battle of the Alamo was a key event in the Texas Revolution.

GOLIAD MASSACRE

After the Alamo, the Mexican army divided into groups and continued marching through Texas. Texans were losing hope. After learning about the defeat at the Alamo, many Texans left their homes to find safety elsewhere. After the battle of Colero Creek on March 20 near Goliad, Texas, the Mexican army forced Texas troops to surrender. Texas soldiers were taken as prisoners of war, but Santa Anna ordered them to be executed instead.

About 340 Texans were executed on March 27, 1836, in what became known as the Goliad Massacre.

REMEMBER THE ALAMO!

In April 1836, Sam Houston and his army marched to Harrisburg, Texas. He learned that Santa Anna's army was nearby. Sam prepared his army for battle. They took cover in a wooded area near the town of Lynchburg. The Texas artillery consisted of two cannons. When Santa Anna's forces arrived, the Texans were ready and a small fight broke out. The Mexicans retreated. The next day, Sam got word that more Mexican forces had joined Santa Anna's army. Sam knew he had to strike quickly. He ordered his soldiers to destroy a nearby bridge to prevent more Mexican soldiers from crossing the San Jacinto River to join Santa Anna.

SAN JACINTO

At 4:00 p.m. on April 21, Sam Houston ordered his attack. The Mexican army was caught by surprise as many of the men, including Santa Anna, were enjoying a mid-afternoon **siesta**. The battle lasted only about 20 minutes. The Texas army lost six men and about 25 were wounded. The wounded included Sam. He was shot in the left leg and the rifle ball shattered his ankle.

Santa Anna was nowhere to be found, so Sam sent out small groups of soldiers to capture him. One group returned with a Mexican prisoner. They did not realize who the prisoner was, though, until other prisoners began calling him "el presidente." They realized then that the Mexican man they had caught was President Santa Anna. Sam hoped Santa Anna's capture would bring an end to the fighting for Texas.

Texas Perspective

Sam was named the hero of the Battle of San Jacinto during which Santa Anna was captured.

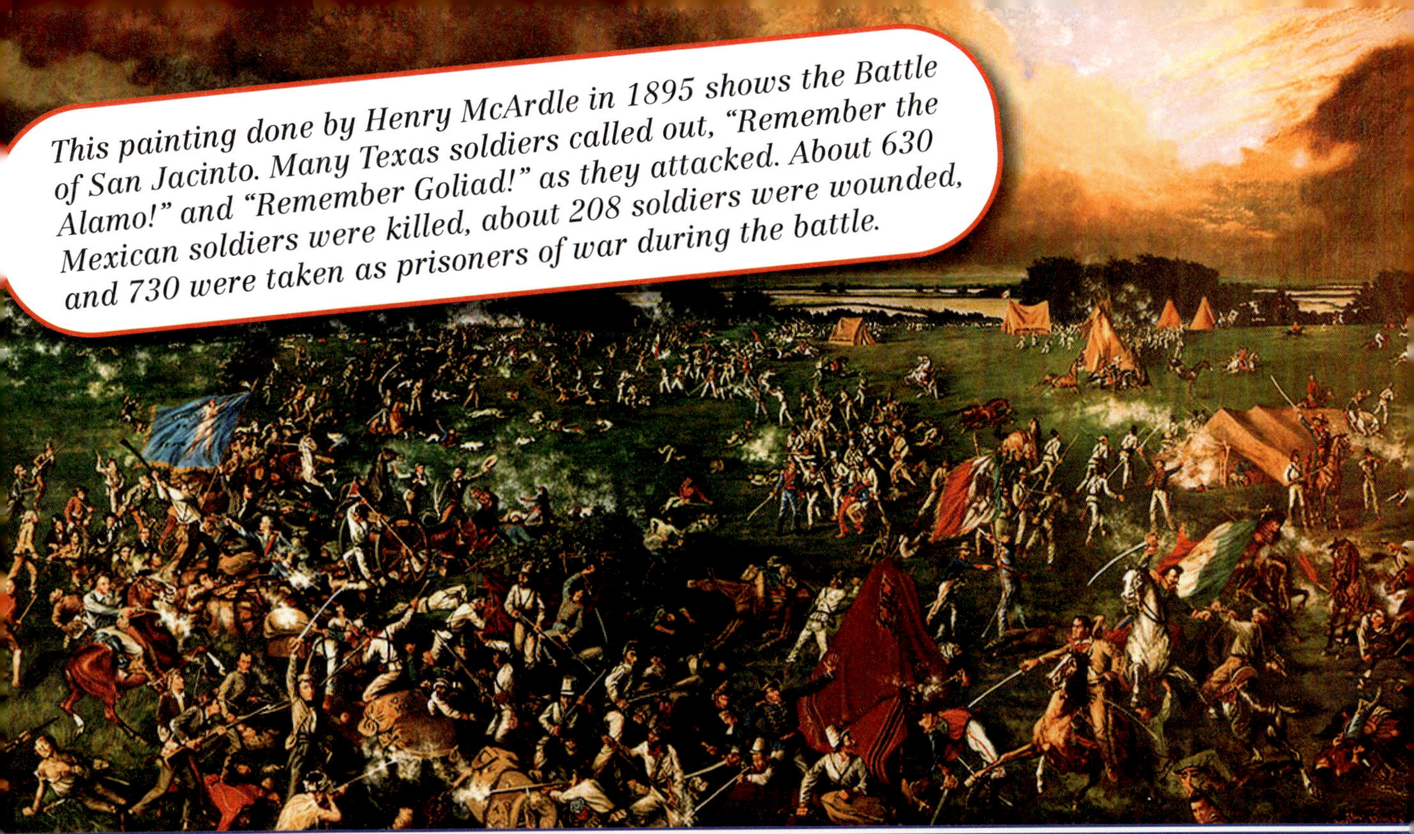

This painting done by Henry McArdle in 1895 shows the Battle of San Jacinto. Many Texas soldiers called out, "Remember the Alamo!" and "Remember Goliad!" as they attacked. About 630 Mexican soldiers were killed, about 208 soldiers were wounded, and 730 were taken as prisoners of war during the battle.

Antonio López de Santa Anna was captured trying to escape the Battle of San Jacinto. This painting shows Santa Anna surrendering to a wounded Sam Houston.

4 PRESIDENT HOUSTON

After the Battle of San Jacinto, Sam's leg wound became much worse and he needed medical attention that was not available in Texas. Sam sailed to New Orleans, Louisiana, and he nearly died on the trip. In New Orleans, three surgeons worked to remove shattered bone in Sam's leg. After his surgery, Sam returned to Texas to help lead the newly independent republic.

LANDSLIDE!

A general election was called for September 5, 1836. Two candidates came forward for the position. The first was Stephen Austin. The second was Henry Smith, who had acted as Texas governor after it declared independence. On August 25, with less than two weeks left before the election, Sam also decided to run for president. As the hero of San Jacinto, he was a favorite with Texans. Sam was elected with a clear majority of votes. Mirabeau B. Lamar, a young soldier who had fought under Sam at the Battle of San Jacinto, was elected vice president.

GOVERNING

Sam Houston was **inaugurated** as president on October 22, 1836. He chose his running mates to be part of his **cabinet**. Henry Smith became Secretary of Treasury, and Stephen Austin was made Secretary of State. Sam moved the government to Houston, Texas, and made the city the capital of the new republic.

Sam Houston ran his government from this Houston building from 1837 until 1839. The building was turned into the Capitol Hotel after the government moved to Austin in 1839.

HOUSTON, TEXAS

John and Augustus Allen were brothers from New York City. They wanted to invest in land and add to their business ventures. They settled near Buffalo Bayou, Texas, on August 30, 1836. They named the town "Houston," because Sam Houston had recently helped Texas gain independence at the Battle of San Jacinto. Sam Houston moved to the city in April 1837 after being sworn in as the first president of Texas. He made Houston the official capital of the Republic of Texas.

By 1837, Houston had a population of 1,500 with more than 100 homes.

PRESIDENT LAMAR

Sam Houston served as president until December 10, 1838. He had to give up his position because the Constitution did not allow him to serve two terms in a row. Sam's vice president, Mirabeau Lamar, won the presidency when the two other candidates died before the election.

During Lamar's presidency, the **currency** used in Texas became nearly worthless. Sam Houston was now serving in the Texas House of Representatives and strongly opposed many of Lamar's policies, especially his treatment of Indians. Lamar drove the Cherokee out of Texas and into Arkansas in 1839 and declared war against the Comanche in 1840.

In 1839, Mirabeau Lamar moved the republic's capital from Houston to Austin, Texas.

THE CHEROKEE

The Cherokee were originally from the eastern United States, around Kentucky and Tennessee. In 1823, the United States government forced them to move westward to Texas. In 1839, Texas president Lamar sent troops to remove the Cherokee from Texas. The two sides fought but the Texas army eventually won and moved the Cherokee from Texas into Oklahoma.

▶*As Americans continued to settle in Texas, the Cherokee and other Indians were pushed out of their traditional territories.*

REELECTED

Sam Houston was reelected as president on December 12, 1841, and replaced Lamar. The Comanche remained at war with Texas until Sam regained power. The Comanche chief trusted Sam and agreed to a peace treaty.

From a letter to Red Bear and Chiefs of the Council, written by Sam Houston October 13, 1842:

> ***"Let the war-whoop be no more heard in our prairies. Let songs of joy be heard upon our hills. In our valleys let there be laughter, and in our wig-wams let the voices of our women and children be heard. Let trouble be taken away far from us; and when our warriors meet together, let them smoke the pipe of peace and be happy."***

COMANCHE

The Comanche Indians lived on the southern plains of the United States, in what is now Kansas, Oklahoma, and Texas. They moved to the area from Wyoming in the 1600s. The Comanche were nomads, which means they moved from place to place. The Comanche lived in tepees. Comanche men were known to be fierce warriors, good hunters, and skilled traders. Comanche women gathered and prepared food.

The Comanche used animal skins and long poles to make their tepees. Tepees were easy to assemble and were light to carry from one place to another.

5 ANNEXATION

During both of Sam Houston's terms as president, he tried to join Texas with another country, such as England, France, or the United States. When a larger, more powerful, or wealthier country adds another country to its territory, it is called annexation. Sam believed annexation would help Texas stay independent from Mexico.

OBSTACLES TO ANNEXATION

Shortly after the Battle of San Jacinto, Sam offered the United States the chance to annex Texas. Leaders of the US government at that time did not want to annex Texas, though. They were worried annexation would start a war between the Unitied States and Mexico.

When Mirabeau Lamar was elected president of the Republic of Texas in 1838, he withdrew the offer of annexation that Sam had made. Lamar was not interested in joining with the United States. The offer to annex Texas was not brought up again until Sam returned to lead Texas in 1841. The United States turned down the offer once more, though.

Texas Perspective

Sam played a leading role in bringing Texas into the United States.

The Republic of Texas allowed slavery. Tom Blue was Sam Houston's slave and bodyguard until 1862.

THE UNITED STATES IN 1845

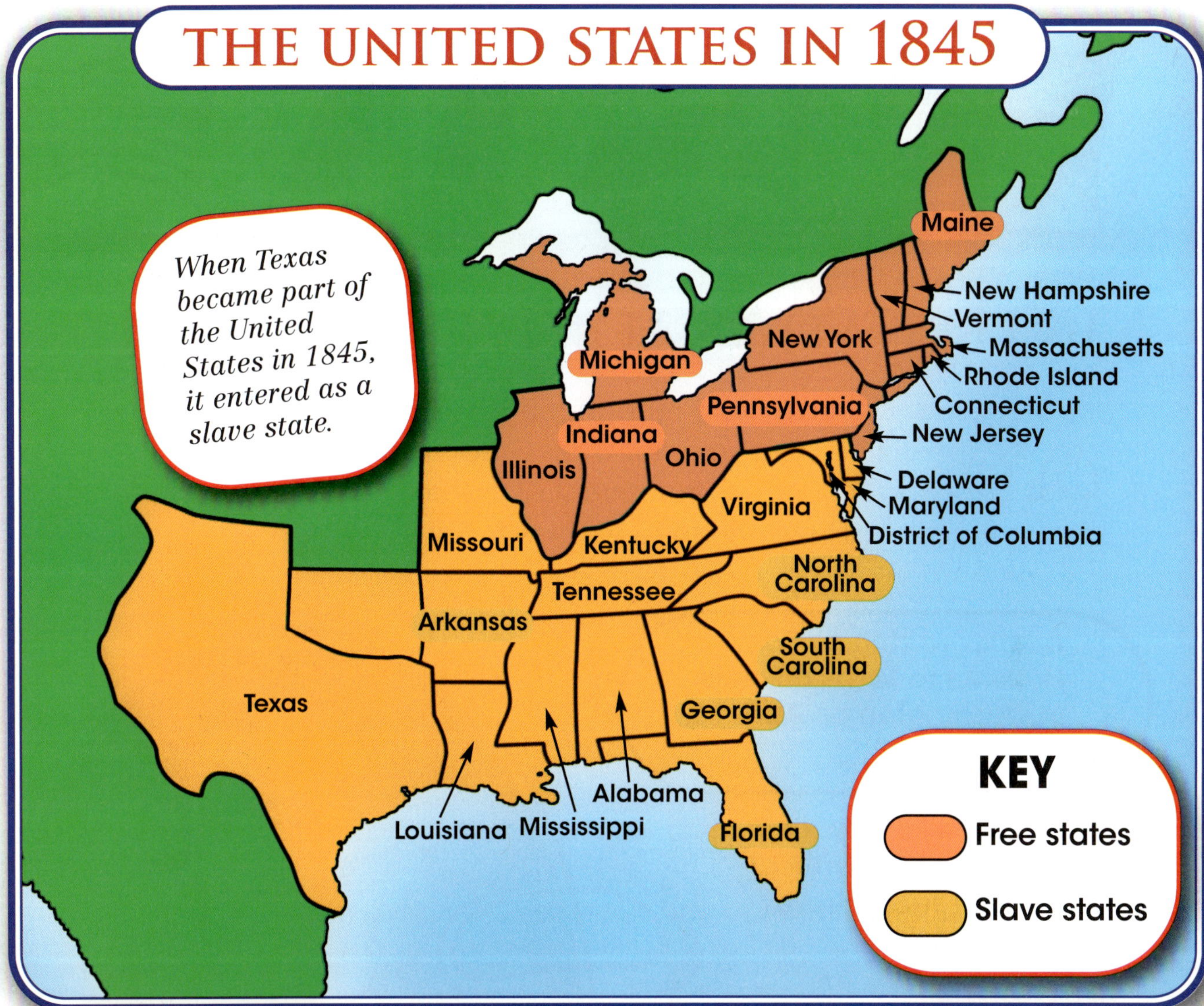

CHANGING THE BALANCE

Another issue that played a role in the annexation of Texas was slavery. During the 1800s, much of the United States was divided over the issue of slavery. By the early 1840s,13 states allowed slavery. These 13 states were known as the slave states. Another 13 states had banned slavery. These states were known as the free states.

Having an equal number of slave states and free states meant that political powers were equal, too. To invite Texas into the Union meant the balance could be weighted toward the slave states. The slave states would then gain political control of the country. Sam Houston believed statehood was best for Texas, though, and hoped the US government would change its mind.

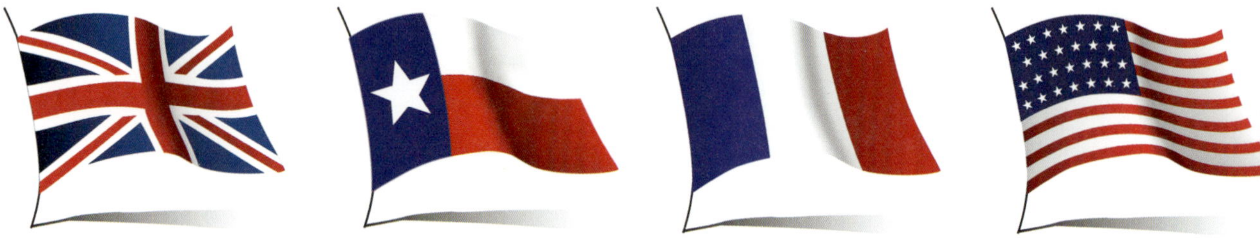

INTERNATIONAL INTEREST

In 1842, Great Britain formally recognized Texas as an independent country. The United States did not want Great Britain to unite with Texas. So John Tyler, the new president of the United States, began to discuss the possibility of annexing Texas with Sam.

A letter written by Sam Houston to Texas officials in Washington on April 16, 1844, states:

"...You may rely upon it, if the Government of the United States does not act immediately, and [conclude] the work of annexation, Texas is forever lost to them... In my opinion, England and France will say to Texas, 'if you will agree to remain separate forever from the United States, we will forthwith prevent all further [trouble] to you from Mexico, and guarantee you Independence.'"

John Tyler agreed with Houston's idea for the United States to annex Texas. Even with many against him, Tyler did whatever he could to try and make that happen.

THE 28TH STATE

In 1844, James K. Polk was elected president of the United States. He supported annexing Texas and continuing slavery. Congress passed a **joint resolution** to annex Texas. The United States would take over the military, postal service, and taxation. Northern Texas would outlaw slavery while southern Texas could continue to allow it if they chose to. The joint resolution was accepted by the congress of the Republic of Texas on July 4, 1845, and a new state constitution was written. On December 28, 1845, Texas became the 28th state of the United States of America.

▲ *James K. Polk was the 11th president of the United States.*

MEXICAN-AMERICAN WAR

Meanwhile, the United States and Mexico were engaged in a long-running dispute over whether the Texas border ended at the Nueces River as Mexico claimed or the Rio Grande as the U.S. claimed. The annexation of Texas led to the Mexican-American War, which lasted from April 1846–February 1848. With the signing of the Treaty of Guadalupe-Hidalgo on February 2, 1848, the U.S. acquired more than 500,000 square miles of land, and established the Rio Grande as the border between the two countries.

On February 19, 1846, president Jones declared, "The Republic of Texas is no more." As he lowered the Texas flag for the final time Sam reached out and collected it.

6 TEXAS POLITICS

Sam Houston continued working in politics after Texas joined the United States. He took a seat in the United States Senate and became one of the first senators from Texas on February 21, 1846. He remained a senator for 13 years.

SENATOR

As senator, one of Sam Houston's main concerns was maintaining a strong union. In the 1850s, southern states, including Texas, were discussing secession. They wanted to form their own country to protect the right to own slaves. Even though Sam owned slaves, he did not want the southern states, especially Texas, to secede over the issue of slavery. Sam believed in keeping the country together at any cost and he publicly spoke out against secession. He voted in favor of **bills** that supported ending slavery. This made Sam unpopular with many people in Texas. The Texas legislature accused him of not serving the interests of Texas.

One of Sam's favorite hobbies was wood carving. He is shown here at a Senate meeting shaving a new piece of wood.

GOVERNOR

Sam ran for governor of Texas in 1857 but lost. He ran for governor again in 1859 and won. On December 21, 1859, Sam took his place as governor of Texas. During his time in office, Sam tried to persuade the people of Texas to not secede from the Union.

In 1859, Sam also ran for the position of United States Democratic Party presidental candidate, but he lost to John Bell (above). John Bell later lost the presidental race to the Republican candidate, Abraham Lincoln.

SECESSION

Most southerners, including those from Texas, did not want Abraham Lincoln to govern them. They believed that Lincoln, and his party's politics, threatened their way of life. A convention to vote on secession began on January 28, 1861. Delegates were elected throughout Texas to decide whether the state would secede from the Union and join the **Confederacy**. Sam knew that Texans were upset, but he continued to stand behind his belief that the South should not break from the Union. He made speeches to convince people in Texas not to secede.

▶*Secession conventions were happening throughout the southern United States at the start of 1861. Sam Houston's birthplace, Virginia, held a convention and decided to secede three months after Texas.*

GOVERNOR NO MORE

Texas delegates voted to secede from the Union on February 1, 1861. In March, Texas joined the Confederacy and reorganized the former state government. Anyone holding political office had to swear an oath of loyalty to the Confederacy. Sam refused to take the oath, so he was thrown out of office as governor on March 16. The Civil War began a little less than a month later, on April 12, 1861.

Abraham Lincoln became the 16th president of the United States on March 4, 1861. Lincoln offered to send the military to force Texas to stay in the Union, but Houston rejected the offer.

TEXAS, TEXAS!

Sam, his wife Margaret, and their eight children moved to their family home in Huntsville, Texas. Sam Houston had given more than 25 years of his life to Texas. Sam's prediction that the Confederacy would be defeated by the Union came true, but he did not live to see it. Sam's health began to fail shortly after the Civil War began. His daughter said that, as Sam lay dying, his last few words were "Texas, Texas! Margaret!" Sam Houston died at his family home on July 26, 1863.

Sam Houston's family home was nicknamed "Steamboat" because of its unusual shape.

6 SAM'S LEGACY

After Sam died, his wife, Margaret, removed from his finger the ring his mother had given him before he joined the army. Inside the ring was engraved the word "honor." Sam Houston had died as he had lived, with honor.

MONUMENTS

Sam was buried in a cemetery in Huntsville, Texas. Ten years later, the state of Texas replaced his gravestone with a much grander one. The stone praises Sam as a brave, fearless, loyal, faithful, devoted, and honest man.

Huntsville, Texas, has the world's tallest statue of an American hero. The 67-foot-tall (20 m) statue of Sam Houston is named "A Tribute to Courage."

Engraved on the memorial is a quote by US president Andrew Jackson that reads: "The world will take care of Sam Houston's fame."

NAMESAKES

Many places in Texas were named after Sam Houston, such as Houston County and the city of Houston. There are also many buildings and landmarks named after Sam, such as the Sam Houston State University, located in Huntsvile, Texas. Huntsvile is also the home to the Sam Houston Memorial Museum, which includes two of the homes Sam lived in while in Texas. They are called the Woodland home and Steamboat House.

Sam is remembered throughout the United States. Other states, such as Missouri, Mississippi, and Minnesota also have cities named Houston. Many American schools outside of Texas also carry Sam Houston's name.

◀ *The San Jacinto Monument is nearly 670 feet (204 m) in height and topped with a huge Lone Star of Texas. The monument is taller than the Washington Monument, in Washington, D.C.*

LEARNING MORE

BOOKS

Gregson, Susan R. *Sam Houston: Texas Hero*. North Mankato, MN: Compass Point Books, 2006.

Woodward, Walter M. *Sam Houston: For Texas and the Union*. New York: Rosen/PowerPlus Books, 2003.

WEBSITES

The Handbook of Texas Online
www.tshaonline.org/handbook

Texas Beyond History
www.texasbeyondhistory.net

HISTORIC SITES

The Alamo
www.thealamo.org

Sam Houston Memorial Museum
www.samhouston.org

San Jacinto Monument and Museum of History
www.sanjacinto-museum.org

TIMELINE

1793 Sam Houston is born in Timber Ridge in Rockbridge County, Virginia, on March 2

1806 Moves to Tennessee with his family

1813 Joins the US Army during the War of 1812

1823 Elected to Congress

1827 Elected governor of Tennessee

1829 Marries Eliza Allen; the marriage lasts only a few months

1832 Moves to Nacogdoches, Texas

1833 Elected as a delegate to the Convention of 1833, and helps write a new Texas constitution

October 2, 1835
Texas Revolution begins with the Battle of Gonzales

March 2, 1836
Serves as a delegate at the Convention of 1836 and appointed as major general of the Texas army; Texas declares independence from Mexico

March 6, 1836
Mexican army attacks the Alamo

April 21, 1836
Leads the Texas army against the Mexican army in the Battle of San Jacinto

October 22, 1836
Serves as president of Texas until December 10, 1838

April 21, 1837
People in Houston celebrate the first anniversary of the Battle of San Jacinto

December 12, 1841
Reelected president of Texas

February 2, 1842
Treaty of Guadalupe-Hidalgo signed

December 29, 1845
Texas becomes the 28th state of the United States of America

February 21, 1846
Becomes senator of Texas

December 21, 1859
Elected as governor of Texas

January 28, 1861
Secession Convention held through February 1. Texas delegates decide to secede from the United States and join the Confederate States of America.

March 16, 1861
Removed from office as governor of Texas because he will not swear an oath to the Confederacy

July 26, 1863
Sam Houston dies in Huntsville, Texas

Texas | Sam Houston

GLOSSARY

Anglo Americans [ANG-gloh *uh-MER-ih-kenz*] American people whose first language is English.
bill [BIL] A draft of a law presented to the legislature, or the law itself.
cabinet [KAB-nit] The group of people elected to advise and work with the president of the United States.
Confederacy [kun-FEH-duh-reh-see] The Confederate States of America; a group of 11 states that seceded from the Union because the Union did not support slavery.
constitution (kon-stih-TOO-shun) The basic rules by which a country or a state is governed.
conventions [kun-VEN-shunz] Assemblies of people meeting for a common purpose.
culture (KUL-chur) The beliefs, practices, and arts of a group of people.
currency [KUR-en-see] Money.
delegate [DEH-lih-get] A person who is chosen to represent a group of people.
go-between [GOH-bih-tween] A person who acts as a link between groups of people to bring about an agreement or help with discussions.
inaugurated [ih-NAW-gyuh-rayt-ed] Officially admitted someone to a political office such as president.
infantry [IN-fun-tree] Soldiers trained, armed, and equipped to fight on foot.
joint resolution [JOYNT reh-zuh-LOO-shun] A resolution passed by both houses of Congress, which then becomes a law.
platform [PLAT-fawrm] Declaration of beliefs and behaviors of a person or group of people.
recourse [REE-kors] Source of help in a difficult situation.
Roman Catholic [ROH-mun KATH-lik] Christian faith or religion in which the Church is run by priests and bishops and the head of the Church is the pope.
seceding [sih-SEED-ing] Withdrawing from, or leaving, an organization.
siesta [see-ES-tuh] Afternoon nap or rest.
Union [YOON-yun] The federal union of states during the time of the Civil War.

INDEX